COMPLETE
CONCERTI GROSSI

Arcangelo Corelli

COMPLETE CONCERTI GROSSI
IN FULL SCORE

DOVER PUBLICATIONS, INC., *New York*

Published in Canada by General Publishing Company, Ltd., 30 Lesmill Road, Don Mills, Toronto, Ontario.

Published in the United Kingdom by Constable and Company, Ltd.

This Dover edition, first published in 1988, is a republication of Volumes 4 and 5 of *Les Oeuvres de Arcangelo Corelli*, edited by Joseph Joachim and Friedrich Chrysander, originally published by Augener & Co., London, ca. 1891.

Manufactured in the United States of America
Dover Publications, Inc., 31 East 2nd Street, Mineola, N.Y. 11501

Library of Congress Cataloging-in-Publication Data

Corelli, Arcangelo, 1653–1713.
  [Concerti grossi, violins (2), violoncello, string orchestra, op. 6]
  Complete concerti grossi.

  For 2 violins, violoncello, and string orchestra.
  Reprint. Originally published: London : Augener, ca. 1891.
Originally published in series: Les oeuvres de Arcangelo Corelli.
  Contents: No. 1 in D major—No. 2 in F major—No. 3 in C minor—[etc.]
  1. Concerti grossi—Scores. I. Title.
M1140.C66 op. 6   1988   87-754627
ISBN 0-486-25606-5

Contents

VORWORT.

Das letzte und grösste Opus von Corelli, welches im December 1712 zu Rom in 7 Stimmen Büchern erschien, war gleich seinen früheren Compositionen mit Hülfe von Nachdrucken schnell in Europa verbreitet; bildete ein Hauptwerk für das damalige grosse Concert und ist von allen um 1710 erschienenen Werken dieser Art das gehaltvollste und lehrreichste.

Bei Corelli ist es klar zu ersehen, dass sich die damaligen Orchesterstücke aus einem Zusammengehen des *Concertino* und des *Concerto grosso* bildeten, d. h. aus der Vereinigung solistischer und chorischer Elemente. Sowohl beim Concertino, wie beim Concerto grosso ist die Bassstimme beziffert, woraus hervorgeht, dass zwei Claviere für die Aufführung benutzt wurden, eins für die drei oberen Solo-Instrumente, das andere für die hinzutretenden vier Ripianisten. Wo es angeht, muss man an einer solchen Praxis festhalten, dann ist die Aufführung dieser Concerte sehr leicht und wird ein grosses Vergnügen bereiten.

Gleich den Sonaten op. 1-4 und den Violin-Soli op. 5 bestehen auch diese Orchester-Concerte aus zwei Abtheilungen, einer ernsteren für das grössere Concert (No. I. bis VIII., Seite 3-170) und einer leichteren, für kleinere Säle (No. IX. bis XII., Seite 171-236).

Die Bedeutung und allgemeine Beliebtheit der Corellischen Musik veranlasste Dr. Pepusch um 1730, sowohl die 48 Sonaten, wie auch diese 12 Concerti grossi bei Walsh in London in Partitur herauszugeben. Dem Titel zufolge geschah solches „sorgfältig" (in Wirklichkeit aber sorglos) und zu dem Zwecke, um diese Stücke „allen Studenten und Ausübenden der Musik" zugänglich zu machen, da sie „von grossem Nutzen" für dieselben seien. Man kann zur Empfehlung dieser zwölf Concerte wohl nichts Besseres beibringen, als die Versicherung, dass der Nutzen, den Pepusch denselben vor 150 Jahren zuschrieb, noch heute besteht. Pepusch hat durch seine Partitur-Ausgabe freilich dazu beigetragen, Corelli's Compositionen zu verdunkeln, denn er setzt die Viola zum Concertino, verwischt also den durch das Ganze gehenden Gegensatz des dreistimmigen Concertino zu dem vierstimmigen Concerto grosso, und giebt ferner dem Concertino-Basse nur dann Ziffern, wenn das Concerto grosso pausirt, während in den gedruckten Stimmen beide Bässe durchgehends beziffert sind. Er machte die letztere Aenderung vielleicht, damit bei der Aufführung mit einem einzigen Clavier auszukommen war. Aber derartige Anbequemungen muss ein Herausgeber der Praxis überlassen und die Werke so drucken, wie der Componist sie geschrieben hat. Die Ausgaben von Pepusch können daher nicht als originalgetreu und zuverlässig angesehen werden.

Fr. Chrysander.

Preface

This last and greatest opus of Corelli, which appeared in print in December 1712* at Rome in seven books, was, like his earlier compositions, rapidly spread over Europe by the aid of reprints, and formed a model for the grand Concerto of its age. Of all the works of this kind written about 1710 it is the most solid and instructive.

In Corelli it is easy to see that the orchestral pieces of his time were formed by a concordance of the Concertino and the Concerto Grosso, or in other words by a union of solo and choral elements. Both in the Concertino and in the Concerto Grosso the bass part is figured, from which it appears that two harpsichords were employed for the performance— one for the three upper solo instruments, the other for the four added ripieno parts. Wherever possible, this practice ought to be maintained; then the production of these Concertos is very easy, and certain to give great pleasure.

Like the Sonatas, Op. 1—4, and the violin Soli, Op. 5, these orchestral Concertos consist of two divisions, the first for the great Concertos (Nos. I—VIII, pp. 3—170), and an easier one for smaller rooms (Nos. IX—XII, pp. 171—236).**

The importance and general popularity of Corelli's music tempted Dr. Pepusch to have the 48 Sonatas, as well as these 12 Concerti Grossi published in score by Walsh in London in 1730. The title says, this was done "carefully"—which is by no means true— and with the object of making these pieces accessible to "all students and practitioners in music, as they were of great advantage" to them. Nothing remains to be added in recommendation of the 12 Concertos, but the assurance that the value which Pepusch assigned to them a hundred and fifty years ago still exists. They are and will remain models of composition in a style which will not become obsolete. But Pepusch himself in his edition did something towards spoiling Corelli's composition, in so far as he puts the viola into the Concertino, thus obliterating the distinction which runs through the whole work, between the Concertino with three instruments and the Concerto Grosso with four, and further figures the continuo bass only when the Concerto Grosso has a pause, whereas in the printed parts both basses are figured throughout. Perhaps he made this last alteration in order that a single harpsichord might suffice for the performance. But anything of this sort ought to be left to be arranged for any performance, and the score should be given as the composer wrote it. The editions of Corelli's works, which Pepusch edited, cannot, therefore, be regarded as reliable and faithful to the originals.

FR. CHRYSANDER.

*Later musicologists have determined that the score was not printed until 1714.
**In the present Dover edition, the pages are 1-169 and 170-235, respectively.

Concerti Grossi
con duoi Violini e Violoncello
di Concertino obligati
e duoi altri Violini, Viola e Basso
di Concerto Grosso ad arbitrio,
che si potranno radoppiare.

Concerti Grossi
for two violins and cello
in the obligatory Concertino
and two more violins, viola, and basso continuo
in the optional Concerto Grosso [*ripieno*],
which may be enlarged.

COMPLETE
CONCERTI GROSSI

Concerto Grosso No. 1

Allegro.

Concerto Grosso No. 1   15

Tutti.

Concerto Grosso No. 2

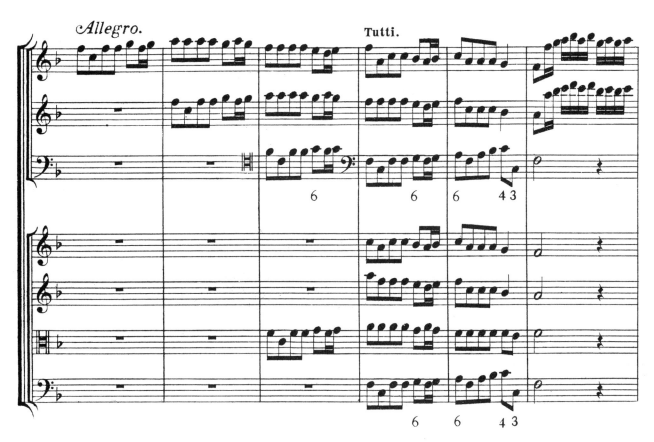

Allegro.

Allegro.

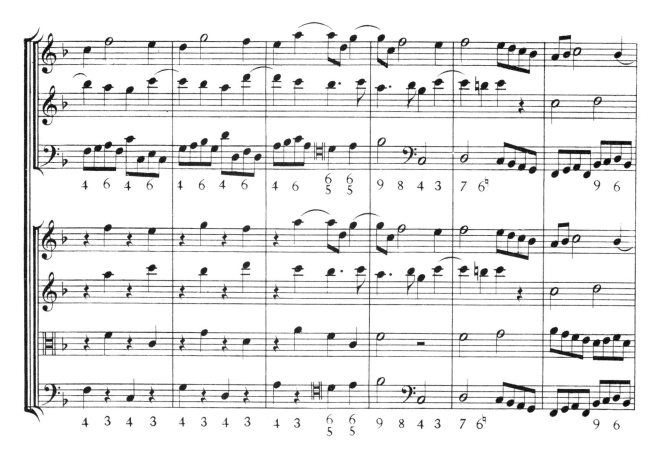

Allegro.

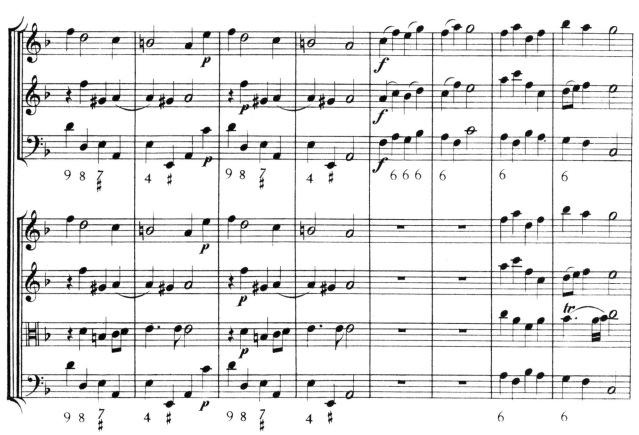

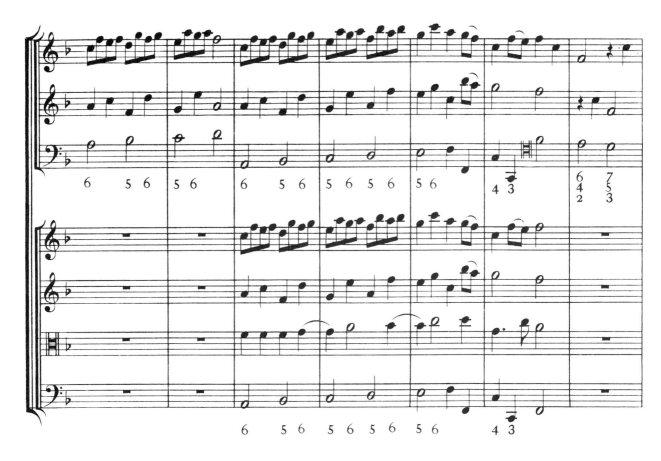

Concerto Grosso No. 3

Tutti.

Vivace.

Tutti.

Concerto Grosso No. 4

Adagio.

74   Concerto Grosso No. 4

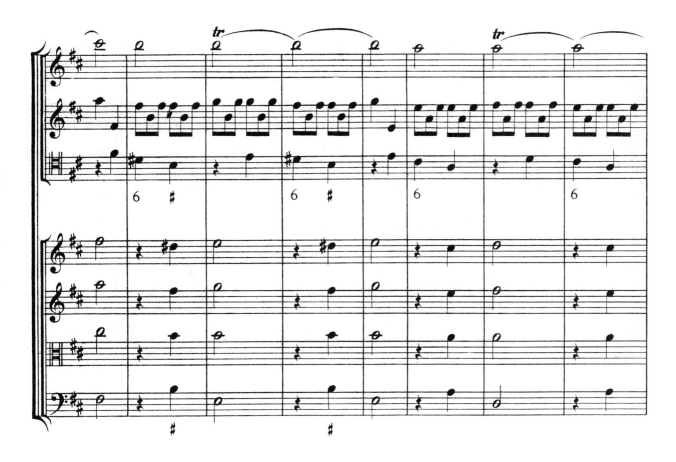

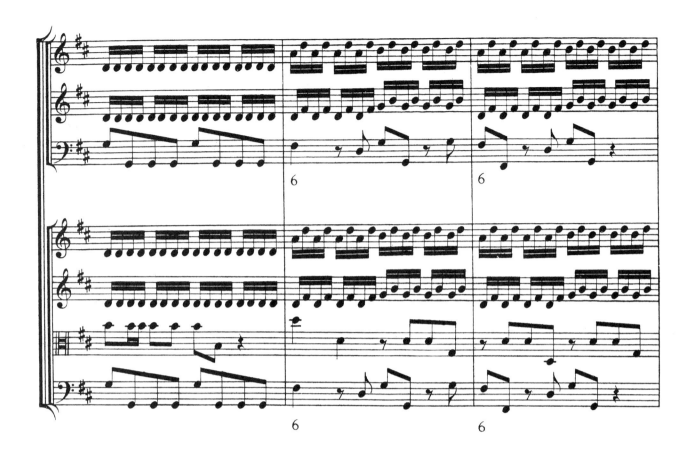

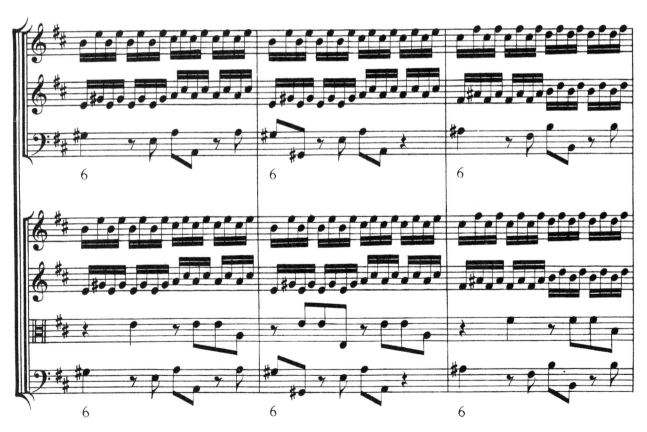

Concerto Grosso No. 5

Largo.

104 Concerto Grosso No. 5

Concerto Grosso No. 6

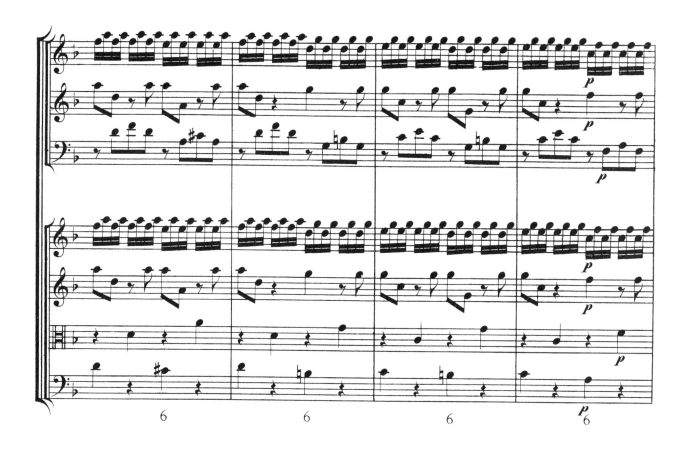

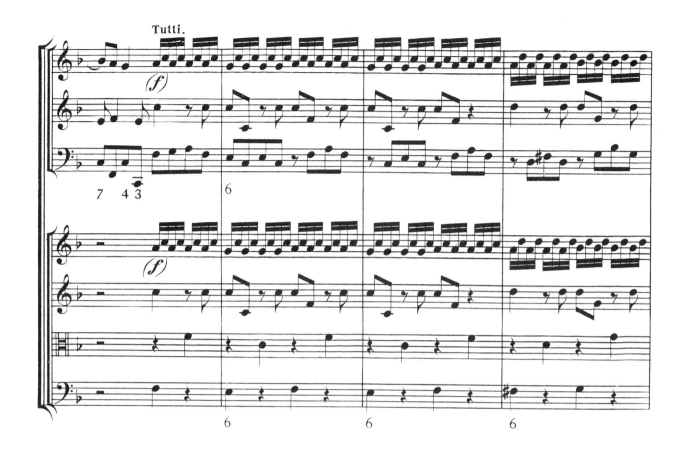

Largo.

114 Concerto Grosso No. 6

Vivace.

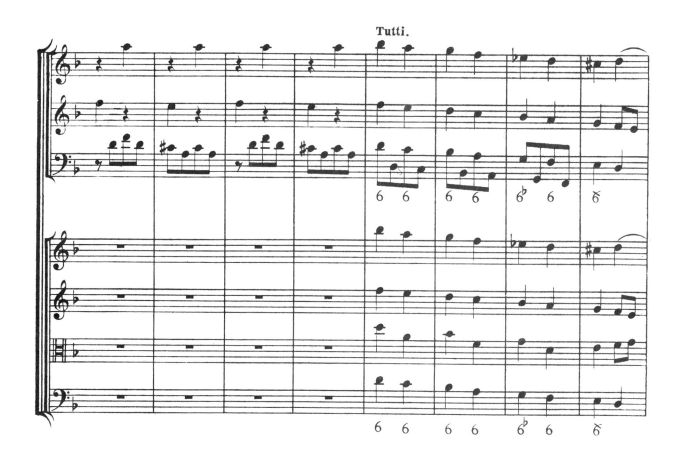

130 Concerto Grosso No. 6

Concerto Grosso No. 7

Allegro.

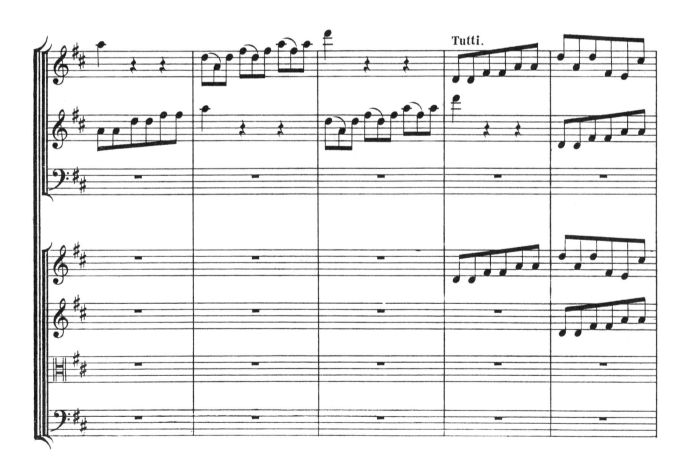

Adagio.

Andante largo.

Vivace.

Soli.

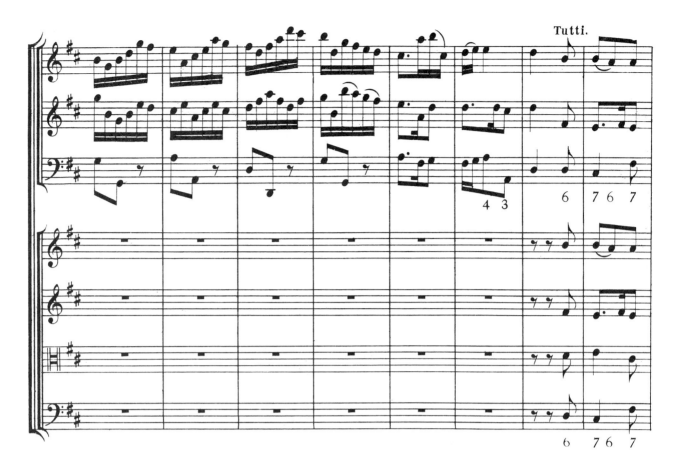

Concerto Grosso No. 8

Fatto per la notte di natale

149

Adagio.

Pastorale ad libitum.

Concerto Grosso No. 9

Preludio

Allemanda

Corrente

Vivace.

Allegro.

Gavotta

Adagio.

Minuetto

Concerto Grosso No. 10

Preludio

Allemanda

Allegro.

Concerto Grosso No. 10 *189*

Adagio.

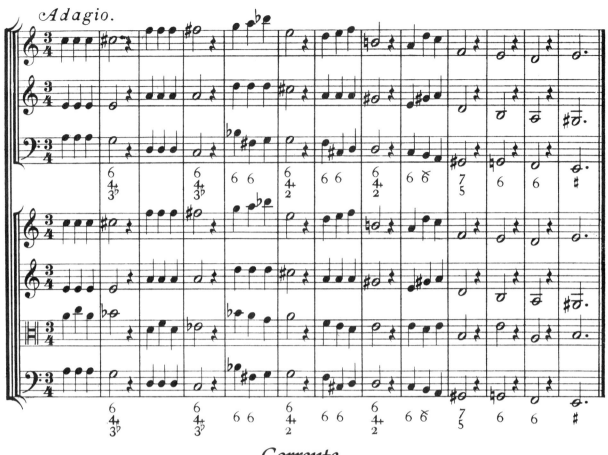

Corrente

Vivace.

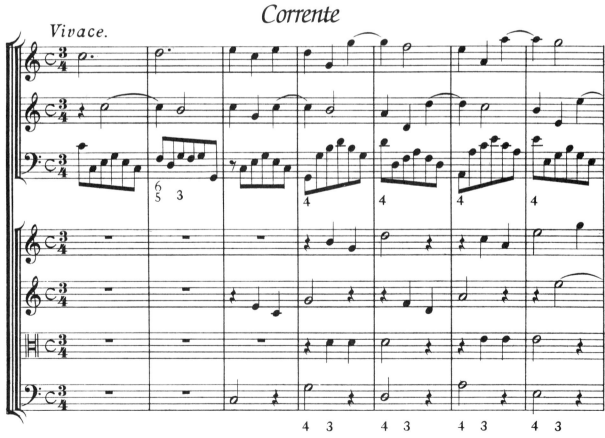

Allegro.

Minuetto

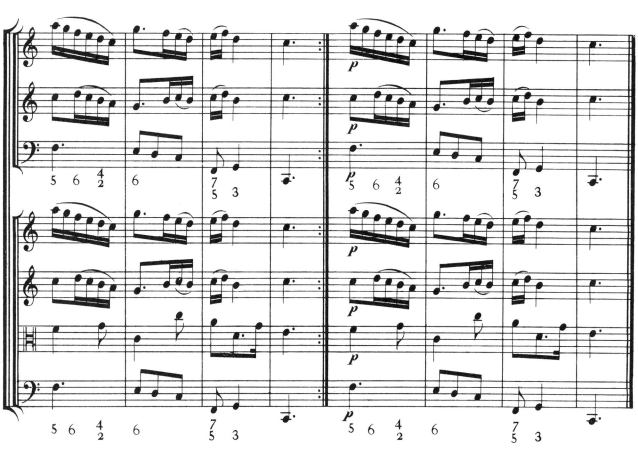

Concerto Grosso No. 11

Preludio

Allemanda

Allegro.

Adagio.

Andante largo.

Sarabanda

Giga

Vivace.

Concerto Grosso No. 12

Preludio

Allegro.

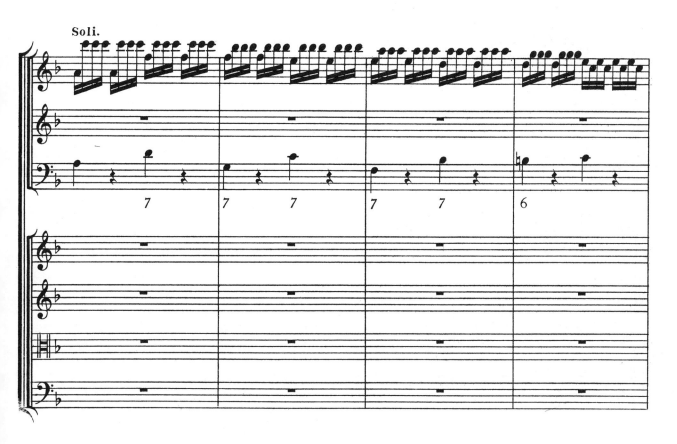

Concerto Grosso No. 12   *223*

Soli.   Tutti.

Adagio.

Sarabanda

Giga